Guiding the Next Generation to Thrive and Build Continued Success for Your Family Legacy

Cliff K. Locks

Dedication

To my wife and our exceptional children, fine students of life, caring, kind, loving, and giving individuals who bring out the best in others.

This book is a heartfelt dedication to the enduring spirit and unwavering love of my beloved father, Richard Locks. I'm saddened by your passing, Aug 25, 2022. Your presence in my life shone as a beacon of strength, wisdom, and limitless support. Under your gentle guidance, I not only imbibed the virtues of perseverance and

compassion, but also developed a deep appreciation for the significance of family, evident in the unbreakable bond shared among my four siblings. You were a loving grandfather of eleven, and two great grandchildren.

Your profound teachings echoed in every corner of my upbringing, reminding me of the invaluable lessons you imparted. You instilled within me the courage to confront life's hurdles with a spirit that refuses to waver.

As I pen these pages, I am reminded of the legacy you've left behind. This dedication is a tribute to you, Dad, an homage to your enduring influence and the cherished memories we created together. Your presence may have transcended the earthly realm, but your essence lives on through the words, actions, and love that you and Mom have shared with us all.

With everlasting love,

Cliff

Copyright Notice

Info@MillionaireLife.Services

© 2023 Millionaire Life Services

ISBN: 978-0-578-26197-3

Table of Contents

Introduction

What does it take to enjoy your lifestyle and maintain inner peace and spiritual strength while also guiding the next generation to continued success? It starts with extensive planning. This planning will be well worth the effort and hard work you put into it. In this book, you will learn how to create a complete and in-depth plan for your entire family and future generations to come. A well-established plan will address possible hurdles along the way that would normally send a family into crisis, however, with a plan, crisis can be avoided, and your family can thrive.

Great wealth impacts families differently, making each family a unique and evolving demographic. These families are often the wealthiest in society, with an accumulation of generational wealth that can be traced back over decades or even centuries. What we have seen is that, with each new generation, comes a set of challenges for which we have compiled a guide of simple steps to follow so you can gain inner peace and live a life of excellence while teaching your children to become happy, capable, and successful adults. You can also ensure that they are aligned with your vision, allowing them to succeed and take the lead in a timely manner when you wish to transfer your company and your wealth to the next generation, continuing the family legacy.

Research points to the many changes occurring within the generations. These challenges will be unique and difficult to navigate. Some leaders are not yet prepared to complete a wealth transfer to their family members. There is also much concern surrounding the successful transfer of the business, and this includes the unique stressors of family wealth. The best successful family businesses run like well-oiled machines because they are composed of individuals who can specialize and focus on the business' fundamentals, all while still embodying a shared mission, values, and vision. The knowledge and skills needed to enable the company to thrive are also present, contributing to that success.

It is critical to identify the different talents in your family and allow everyone to succeed in their area of expertise. In some families, you will see that some in the second generation may want nothing to do with the family business but want to share in the financial benefits from that organization. You will learn that there is a necessary balance to reach for while playing your own important role in the business. This balance will surround the need to maintain goodwill while distributing the responsibility of the business along with shared wealth. This can be a daunting task for anyone, but especially if you are in a leadership role.

For the sake of an example, let's assume that the first generation started the business and had four children. On one hand, you are proud that child one may be interested in continuing the family business, having high hopes to take it over one day. However, on the other, you may not think that he/she exhibits the best ability and skills to do the job. Your love is present, but you are concerned for the family legacy. Then, you have child number two, who aspires to be a doctor or lawyer. The third child may choose to live halfway across the world, following their calling to devote themselves to aiding in a solution to cure world hunger. The fourth may be an incredibly talented and creative artist who wants to enjoy life, create beautiful art, and relax with their family, with no desire to work directly with the family business, let alone be the captain at the helm.

All may be loving and devoted children, and each make you proud as a parent. While the answers may seem obvious to you, they may not seem equal or fair to the second generation. Making this decision more complicated is the conflicted emotions that are created in the process as you strive to a make smart and successful decision. A wise businessperson may struggle because all four in the next generation may be solid individuals, and yet, the only one interested in continuing in your footsteps may have great challenges ahead. Throughout this book, we will address those very challenges, offering you a guide to navigate the complicated road to a successful succession of wealth and business.

Family businesses dominate worldwide, however, many of them falter or stop working altogether, and the success ends at the succession of the company. Handing over the reins to the second generation suddenly becomes risky and the foundation you built begins to shake. Going the distance in the third generation has even less success probability. To maintain the growth and sustainability of these enterprises, we must recognize and support individual talents within our families. It's important to recognize what each member offers their abilities geared towards success and the contribution to the business, along with any added substantial benefits they bring to the table. After years of devotion, and when a business becomes successful, the family will strive to continue for generations. There is often a good combination of financial planning, business, arts, humanities, and philanthropy and multiple ways in which to tie them together. These all play a huge role in growing a diverse business, while involving every person's individual interest and strength.

It's a delicate balance between confidence in knowing that you are on the right track and having patience and compassion to continue your journey towards gaining inner peace. This book focuses on different topics that we have found to be helpful to use as guides along the way. The subjects are designed for Very High

Net Worth (VHNWI) families and the Ultra-High Net Worth Individuals (UHNWI) to ultimately guide you to become a more accomplished partner, parent, mentor, leader and generally a genuinely more accomplished and complete person. Remember, the goals you have set for yourself in life enabled you to achieve great success. This book will encourage you to lead the way, not only toward *your* continued future success, but in leading by example and becoming a steward, you will successfully inspire the future generations to proceed forward confidently with a solid plan in place.

1

Integrating Family into the Family Business

We have all experienced, or heard about, the search for meaning. This search often goes well beyond financial success. Many people feel destined to achieve remarkable things, be it in innovation, generous humanitarian efforts, or global impact. The goal is to leave the world with something more than they entered. Countless individuals work their entire lives to achieve what many find elusive. Toward the end of our journey, it has become clear that the true meaning and purpose we seek to improve the world is often based on our connections to other people and our desire to create a positive legacy.

The beginning of fundamental connections starts with the immediate family. While we always love our children, many in the younger generation will share different ideas, and have varying thought processes that differ from your own. They may have different goals, values, and outlooks on life than their parents have. The Baby Boomer generations (1st and 2nd born from 1946 to 1964) certainly had different outlooks than their parents at the time. Gen X (from 1965 to 1980) are following their path, as it should be. The value of listening to and learning from the younger generations is enormous because they have their finger on the pulse of what is yet to come. The wisdom from the generation before cannot be overlooked, however.

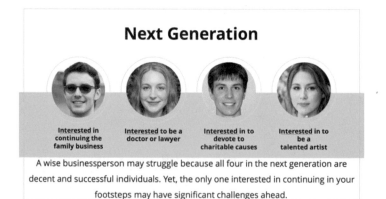

Next Generation

| Interested in continuing the family business | Interested to be a doctor or lawyer | Interested in to devote to charitable causes | Interested in to be a talented artist |

A wise businessperson may struggle because all four in the next generation are decent and successful individuals. Yet, the only one interested in continuing in your footsteps may have significant challenges ahead.

The problem often arises in the fact that the younger generation may not recognize or appreciate our knowledge. We're up against things like Google and YouTube, and while they may not have all the answers, they offer a lot, causing our wisdom to be considered useless. Most searches will allow anyone access to top business, investment marketing materials, industry blogs, and reports for anyone who wishes to gain a wealth of information in record speed. You've got to understand that, according to research, the average attention span of Gen Z is 8 to 12 seconds. This generation will not wait for a browser to open and considers it a broken link at just five seconds of a delay caused by buffering. Additionally, they can work on an average of three to five screens at a single time.

COMMUNICATION IS KEY

Sharing our wisdom with the next generation means combining our knowledge of what has worked in the past with their knowledge of what the future holds. We must listen with our ears and have an open, well-intentioned heart. This ensures we all learn and share insights while being heard and appreciated. It is an opportunity to have equal open-ended communication and allows long-held values, standards, and ideals to be shared. This communication also provides innovative space to incorporate new ideas, providing futuristic visions, the fertile ground needed to grow and prosper.

Most often, when it comes to our family wealth and business, we would prefer the future generation to share our values and continue our legacy the way we began it. The shared purpose can be nurtured to serve as the guide and a predication over the long term to successfully agree on the infinite number of decisions that inevitably need to be made. It takes bending and compromising so families can remain united while still sharing values, albeit in a more open form of communication that allows every member to participate. There is a balance that every generation can achieve.

Everyone benefits when this is done accurately and successfully. Without allowing that open form of communication, many families, parents, siblings, and extended family members often take on oppositional sides and can become resentful. Distance grows, eventually leading to emotional, professional, and financial distance and fractured relationships. Unless the path forward is changed and adjusted accordingly, the business and wealth transfer will falter and fail.

UNDERSTANDING THE DIFFERENT GENERATIONS

Today's workforce boasts four generations. These generations are very different and have equally different experiences that impact how they view the world—personally and in business. Arguably, Generation X was the first generation that caused an incredibly meaningful change in how business was conducted. Computers, smartphones, and instant access ushered in the ability to adapt to change quickly. Each generation brings differing talents, wisdom, and abilities to the table. Each generation is needed if the legacy of success in one's family is to continue.

An example can be found in the contrast of the Baby Boomer Generations and Millennials (born between 1981 and 1996). Baby Boomers have gained years of business expertise, but struggle moving their businesses forward because, often, they do not adapt easily technologically. This is mainly due to the fact things shift so quickly now. On the other hand, Millennials (as most frequently referred to in the Northern Hemisphere but are also known as

Gen Y.1 and Y.2) grew up with instant gratification due to online shopping, social media, and the ability and access to the latest news all in the palm of their hands. They are more often tech-savvy consumers that need what they want, within 24 hours or less, and expect that to be true every time.

In 2022, Millennials are still the largest population on earth, composing close to 22% of people. There are currently more digital-savvy people on earth who have no recollection of life without instant access to products, information, or knowledge. Millennials are now also the largest and most educated generation globally and quickly becoming the most influential. This fact means that the political, economic, social, and environmental terrain will be greatly changed in the next several decades to come. In the natural progression in the world, Baby Boomers will soon cease to be the most influential generation.

2

Mastering a Multi-Generational Family Business

Contrary to what most people think, we are not actually witnessing a major generational gap in the workplace. It presently boasts four different generations, with different thought processes and different talents. Those born after 1996, Gen Z, are making their way into the workforce, and Millennials are inheriting the corporate world. We must now ask what the best way to keep businesses flourishing with multi-generations in play is? There is no magic solution to survival in this ever-changing economy. The best organizations will be flexible and innovative with all their practices; they will optimize various skill sets and perspectives and learn how to recognize and adapt to world fluctuations. They will not resist change, but ultimately create it.

Having a family business that thrives is a goal that is attainable. When guides are followed, and if hearts, minds, and ears remain open between generations, working cohesively together, they can create a dynasty. A key factor in this is the important step of allowing the younger generation to be empowered to make great strides that bring forth innovative ideas. All of this is done, while allowing the older generation to play an equally key role in mentoring the younger generation with experienced wisdom to bring those ideas to market and mesh them successfully into the business. Going forward, this is a worthy endeavor. While not easily accomplished, it is possible to bring the company to greater heights and enable the family to become a stronger, more cohesive unit to achieve a highly sustainable level of success.

The truth is that many families have mastered a multi-generational family business successfully. However, some generations butt heads between elder parents and their now-adult child(ren). Success begins early on, often when generation two is in primary school. The kids should be exposed to age-appropriate business knowledge by gaining access to the monumental effort parents put into the business. It continues from the early years and goes into more depth, during high school and college years, when the child is no longer a child and can learn exactly how the business succeeds in a more detailed way.

An adult should be transparent, explain the *what, how,* and *why,* and give open and honest feedback to the second generation. The eventual sharing of control equates to success as the family business moves forward. If there are secrets or hidden agendas, no transparency or shared vision, the relationships will be compromised, and the business' future is at risk.

The Risk of Not Maintaining Familial Relationships

At the VHNWI and UHNWI levels, it is more than relationships or businesses at risk; great generational wealth may falter. While you may have worked all your life to create a wonderfully fulfilling business and personal life for your family, it is important to be open and amenable to maintaining a close and healthy relationship with your family. The work-life balance will not mean much if it is all about work. When you encourage your children's creativity, they will often find the drive and determination you had as a child. Given that base, you create an empire that can grow and thrive. Passing on the wealth, without the drive to grow and create more success, and to act in a philanthropic manner by giving back, is just handing wealth down to allow the next generation to spend it and live a comfortable life without continuing the efforts you were raised and committed to reaching. The legacy you are building today may not be one that continues tomorrow.

While having an inheritance passed down to children may be what they "want or expect," many successful family businesses have shared their thoughts on how important it is to be fully accessible and teach the shared values they most hold dear. By doing this, it will allow the next generation to continue to feel creative, driven, successful, and valued. These solid work ethics, morals, and values need to be taught early on. Your work ethic needs to be passed onto the second generation and beyond. If the first generation only passes on the wealth without the ethics and the desire to continue the shared mission to grow the business, the second generation may spend it, and the third may see none of it. Along with the shared mission, the next generation is raised to continue and grow the business, and they will teach their children, who will then learn to carry it forward to succeed. If the mindset is not taught early on, it will be difficult, if not impossible, to sustain the wealth.

Blending Your Values with Your Children's

There is a special key to keeping harmony in the family and guaranteeing success in the family business for future generations. That key is learning to blend your values with that of your children's. You can do this by valuing their ideas and teaching them, by example, how you created your success. You cannot expect them to be your clone, but you can help them to understand your work ethics, and at the same time, listen with an open mind to their ideas as well.

Keeping the business conversations separate from the family sets up a void for future generations to succeed, no matter how good your intentions may have been. What your children learn at home and in observing you in the business world is equally as important as higher education. This hands-on education, and the value and importance it provides, is truer now than at any time in the past.

Connection is where that hands-on education starts. You may set up a solid relationship early by sharing a hobby or even coaching your child's sports team, such as soccer, baseball, basketball, or Lacrosse. Mixing business and pleasure may mean taking your kids with you to a tradeshow event or conference and then going skiing, playing tennis, horseback riding, boating, or sailing afterward. I could mean going to a business event and then visiting the museums or enjoying the arts, which may include painting, singing, ballet. Or or might mean going to concerts, together, enjoying the theater and introducing them to your experiences with playing an instrument, or learning to fly a plane. Participating with your children regularly as they take up an interest in these areas will create a lifelong bond, which can carry forward as they progress into showing an interest in the business.[1]

Jaffe, D. (2018, August 30). *If you want your family business to last several generations.* Forbes. Retrieved March 26, 2022, from https://www.forbes.com/sites/dennisjaffe/2018/08/30/if-you-want-your-family-business-to-last-several-generations/?sh=58e3b5 0f7c16

3

Your Children's Role in the Business

When is it time to discuss bringing your children into the business? The answer is "Now." Start today by sharing the business with them. Allow them to see you in action, let them recognize how to make good decisions by your example, and allow them to share their creative ideas with you. Each child is unique and brings special abilities, skills, and personality to the table. We love our children equally and dearly, and it's natural to desire that they feel a similar passion for the company you built. Meeting them where they are at is necessary. Understanding your child for the unique individual they are means you learn in ways to communicate that best suits their communication needs and styles.

The Benefits of Early Childhood Assessments

Let us touch for a moment on the special needs child. Many parents did not and still do not want or believe in "labeling" a child as learning differently. All children learn at different speeds, and just as all raw kernels of popcorn in a container may look alike and be the same size, they all pop at various times. Children bloom at different times throughout life and measuring, or labeling is not necessarily helpful. However, in seeing the child that is not making milestones on a timely basis, it is important not to ignore or wait too long to seek out early interventional services (between birth and three years of age) because early intervention can make an enormous impact on a child's future success. If you or your child's pediatrician feels that certain milestones such as smiling, making eye contact, rolling over, sitting unassisted, first words, crawling, etc., are not where they could/should be, please do not let a label or fear of judgment be an obstacle to seeking support for your child. The health and wellbeing of your children always comes first to business or other obligations. Stigmas shouldn't be what stops you from supporting your children's future to the fullest.

When trying to navigate your family life, keep in mind that the earlier you intervene, the faster your child will improve to grow into their own abilities, and the less they will fall behind. It is not easy to accept that on your journey into life with children, it may not be exactly what you envisioned it to be, but the grace in parenting is in learning to accept what is and doing the best you can to make a life for them, the best it can be. Do not just seek out one opinion from a doctor or teacher. Seek out opinions from top pediatric neuropsychologists, speech pathologists, occupational therapists, or physical therapists and get the help your child may need. When caught and treated early, many childhood obstacles are left in the rear-view mirror (and not even recalled by the child between birth and three years of age). The fact that you supported them will forever be present in their daily lives and as they chase their dreams in the family company. If the need continues into primary school and later, do whatever it takes to improve the situation, because ignoring it is not the answer. A child's confidence stems from overcoming challenges, not hiding from them. Help them know there is no harm in reaching out for help. The saying, "It takes a village," is true when it comes to raising children, and seeking out the true specialists in your "village," will greatly enhance your child's future.

Lean into Change

Please think of the changes we have seen over the last seven decades. Now, think of us, laughing at our parents trying to implement the time clock on their VCR. They did not know how to set the clock, and we laughed at them. Look at all the new avenues for advertising, social media, apps, and so much more. We must admit that it is a new world, and the next generation will lead us into it. We can, in a cohesive family, learn from each other. To do so, is not only wise, but enhances that bond between family members.

A good example is found in Mark Cuban of Shark Tank. Recently, Mark invested $400K in a young female entrepreneur after initially backing away from the deal because it was not in his wheelhouse. Please read this article and watch the video all the way to the end, where Mark explains why he invested with Tania to his fellow Sharks.[2] In the end, Mark wanted to help not just Tania; he wanted her to meet and mentor his daughters (ages 14 and 17) and asked Tania to share her passion with his teenagers about her experience and determination in business. Mark's voice cracks (which you rarely witness with Mark), and in that one moment, one realizes, he is a wise man, a father, who recognized that perhaps he was not inspiring his teenage daughters as once hoped, so he found a workaround, and asked this young 19-year-old, Tania, to help him inspire his girls. As the other Sharks look at

Mark with questioning eyes, a shocked Barbara Corcoran asks, "Mark, what made you change your mind and come back in?" He replied, "In the end, I saw my kids in her (Tania), and every father has aspirations for their kid, and you know if I can get her (Tania) to connect to my kids, that's more important than the money involved."

Baruch, Y. (2022, January 23). 19-year-old beauty entrepreneur lands a deal with Mark Cuban. Black Enterprise. Retrieved March 26, 2022, from https://www.blackenterprise.com/entrep reneur-tania-speaks-19-lands-a-deal-with-mark-cuban/

Mark is a prime example of doing whatever you can to teach your child valuable work ethics. Directly or indirectly, helping someone to succeed, to learn to overcome obstacles, to rise and meet the challenge is an invaluable life lesson. The best way to do this is by connection. So many parents, even the wealthiest of parents, find it hard to connect with their children. Sometimes, it's about finding who you need to help you inspire your children, mentor them, and help to instill those values at an early stage. By doing this, you are positioning them to grow in a good place, mentally, physically, personally, and in business.

4

Teaching the Value of Goal Setting

When you hire a top executive to aid in overseeing your business, you will probably interview several young potential managers, perhaps the same age as your own children. You may believe them to be more experienced, better situated to the position, and to have abilities that surpass those currently of your adult child. Because of this, you may feel that by offering them more support and encouragement is necessary while you take them under your wing. Perhaps, you believe them to have greater experience and even drive than you own adult child, and they may very well have all of that and more.

However, your experience, trust, and visions for the future of your company, combined with your children's knowledge, can merge into a strong alliance, one stronger because of that familial bond. It could give greater confidence, trust, and shared desires to bring success to the next generation and allow your family business to not only succeed, but thrive, and at the same time, create an impenetrable bond between you and your family. This choice can build a legacy that not only you, but future generations, to come aid in continuing to build upon. It will take some extra effort because you are a family, and you will be mixing business and home life at the end of the day. It becomes a 24 -hour think tank of sorts. It can be difficult to separate business from emotions, which is necessary if you are looking to mentor the next generation successfully.

When guiding your children toward finding their place in the family business, the most important aspect to remember is the gift of guiding them on how to set goals. Future goals work as momentum and are the driving force on the journey of success. By aiding your children in setting future goals, you should keep in mind the shared goal of familial success. A child's untapped potential can give them a world of possibilities to be successful if they know, and keep in sight, what their goals are.

Goal Setting Exercise

One exercise you can do with your child is to set annual goals together—family, business, and personal goals that include them. Then, help them set age-appropriate goals they can work towards throughout the year. Goal setting keeps a young child, adolescent, teen, or young adult focused. It keeps them on a course toward a happy future. In the beginning, you may need to encourage some simple goals for a very young child, such as:

1. I will do chores to earn an allowance each week. My chores include maintaining my bedroom, helping in the kitchen, putting out the garbage, feeding the dog or cat, etc.

2. I will save ½ of my allowance for the long term in a bank or brokerage account.

3. I will allow myself to spend or save 25% of my allowance toward a researched and planned purchase for something I want and have permission to buy.

4. I will donate 25% of my allowance to a worthwhile cause, such as an animal shelter or food pantry.

5. I will (name something, i.e., get a B in Math, join a team sport, get a part-time job, stop biting my nails, snow ski) by the end of the year.

Have a dedicated book kept in a safe place, just for setting down goals. Next to each goal, leave space to the right to put a checkmark and a date the goal was accomplished. Along with that book, make a copy of those goals to post on their bathroom mirror or bedroom door—some place they can see it as a daily reminder that they created goals they alone can achieve. One of our sons used a write-on wipe-off board in his room. As simple as this seems, it's proven to be successful. He also cut picture out of magazines of homes he liked, or of items he wanted to purchase later in life.

Have your children sit down with you (in the beginning years) annually or semi-annually, then move to quarterly to update their goals. The goals should get more challenging as children get older and include what grades they want to earn, what subjects would be interesting, what they might like to excel in, what position you would like to see them hold in your business, the mentors that could provide guidance on their journey, the colleges they may want to attend, and any other matters that are important to put in their goals.

Helping a child in this manner can also be accompanied by positive affirmations. Teach these to your children, say them with them, and have it become part of their daily routines. This can be a mantra or meditation if you will. You can make it whatever you please. Below, are some examples:

1. I am strong. I am smart. I am capable. I have big dreams and goals I can achieve.

2. I can do this independently, but I can also ask someone if I need help.

3. Some days may be challenging, but I am strong, and tomorrow will be a new day; I can and will meet those challenges.

4. I am a good person, and I will be good to others.

5. If someone does something that upsets me, I will talk about it, but in the end, I will behave the way I was taught to behave in challenging situations.

6. Every day, and in every way, I am getting better and better with practice.

7. Life is 10% of what happens to me and 90% of how I react to it; I have the power within me.

5

Philanthropic Endeavors and Their Importance in Your Family

Business longevity correlation may have to do with the fact that philanthropy gives family business members a sense of purpose. Philanthropy can be both rewarding but also smart for business. Remember the second generation with four different children who had four different outlooks on their futures? Philanthropic endeavors can tie into so many areas and allow a family business to give back to world health, the arts, global environmental impact, and allows family members to connect with the business on that level.[3] It's a way of offering an olive branch to your children, providing them the avenues needed to contribute in ways that bring meaning to them. It allows them the ability to have enriched lives both in meaning, the family business, and your legacy.

One of the most important aspects of your life is giving back. Because it feels good to give back, the rewards of doing so are truly limitless. Philanthropy is not only important to society, but it is also crucial to your mental and emotional health. Philanthropy is also a way to promote the family's values. Your charitable contributions are an investment in the spiritual, psychological, and even physical well-being of your family and the community. Studies have shown that givers gain significantly from the act of giving. Giving back is also one of the best ways to unite your family in fulfilling your responsibilities in building a positive family legacy. When you build family traditions into giving, you provide your loved ones with the daily spiritual and physical enrichment they desperately need. Having that child represent your company in areas that they are passionate

---

Hatcher, R. (2021, October 28). *Everything you wanted to know about philanthropy but were afraid to ask.* LinkedIn. Retrieved March 26, 2022, from https://www.linkedin.com/pulse/everything-you-wanted-know-philanthropy-were-afraid-ask-robyn-hatcher

about keeps them involved in your business, making you both proud and fulfilled.

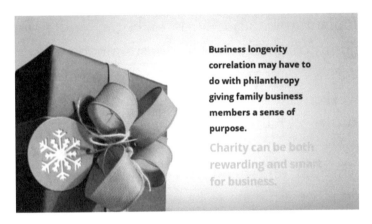

Business longevity correlation may have to do with philanthropy giving family business members a sense of purpose.

Charity can be both rewarding and smart for business.

In this "me generation," the current levels of uncertainty are made more challenging as we continue through a pandemic like our generation has never seen. It stresses the importance now, more than ever, for philanthropic endeavors. It's critical that open communication is all part of any philanthropic endeavor. Along with those very important things, is the equally important need for leadership qualities that you should exemplify in the present and in the future.

Philanthropy as a Sustainable Means of Success

Philanthropy also needs to be an option for family companies looking for sustainable success across generations. The older generation worked hard, saved all their lives, gave to well-known charities, and set up continuous generational giving. However, the Millennials who did not spend years earning and saving great wealth seem to be much more direct as to how they want to give back and focus on grassroots organizations or social endeavors aimed toward specific areas of highly publicized organizations to create change in the world. There has been a definite shift toward sustainability, social responsibility, and environmental causes. A balance can be found here when discussing how the family should invest in philanthropy.

When you create family traditions into giving, you provide your loved ones with daily spiritual and physical enrichment they desperately need.

Setting an example is where it all starts. The benefits are immeasurable when the parents and grandparents set the example of being strong and steady leaders and role models for the rest of their family. Leading by example is crucial in maintaining a healthy family life and a prosperous corporation. Leadership is seen through one's ability to transfer ideas, beliefs, attitudes, and values toward a goal, such as philanthropy, to help everyone progress into the future. The obvious goal is to allow each family member the opportunity to go forth and thrive. They should feel supported as they go forward to live a successful and fulfilling life, have children of their own, and teach the 3rd and 4th generations the same values while continuously giving back in a philanthropic manner. That allows for a happy family and a multi-generational successful business along with major philanthropic endeavors.

Avoiding the Pitfalls of
Generational Wealth

To guarantee their continued success, successful multi-generational families often have guidelines for the company's continuity outlined in their trusts or wills. Both a trust and a will contain a list of beneficiaries. Many are written with strategies that include directives to help maintain the wealth over many generations to prevent it from being squandered by one individual or family or many families in a generation. It is done with the desire to keep family values, business strategies, and visions, such as philanthropy, in mind. It is an overall management approach to maintain and grow wealth in the future. It is, in effect, set up to keep an eye on and help continue to guide the next several generation(s) forward by implementing wise decision-making to help balance the equation for generations beyond. There is often a third-objective wealth-management company whose sole purpose is to ensure the will or trust is carried out in the way it is intended.

There are several factors that any multi-generational family should consider when thinking about their will or trust. Take into consideration the possibility of the scenario in which one generation believes in passing on all the family's wealth to the next generation without passing along the clear values, strategies, wisdom, and ability to be successful. In that case, they may not successfully pass on the wealth comfortably if there are subsequent generations. This is setting the family and its legacy up for failure.

Here is why that is so often true: when the first generation passes, some do not thoroughly plan how future money is to be spent, and they may not leave directives in place for continuity. There may not be enough assets left over to provide for all beneficiaries equally unless there are specific instructions and directives on how to maintain the wealth. When the succession of a family business and generational wealth does not have a plan that is specially critiqued to address these issues, the family will be thrown into chaos, and often bickering will weaken the familial bond, not to mention the chaos created in the family business.

Take the Vanderbilt Family, an example of generational wealth, which was sadly bound to fail without clear direction. Everyone needs the desire to achieve something. It often has a disastrous outcome if you pass along the wealth without imparting the values, drive, knowledge, trust, and advance directives as you transition your wealth. This is why there is so much emphasis put on a foolproof plan to prevent a legacy such as the Vanderbilt family experienced.[4]

---

[4] Robehmed, N. (2019, June 17). The Vanderbilts: How American Royalty lost their Crown Jewels. Forbes. Retrieved March 26, 2022, from https://www.forbes.com/sites/natalierob ehmed/2014/07/14/the-vanderbilts-how-american-royalty-lost-their-crown-jewels/?sh=791b5d7c353b

Preventing Pitfalls

We've discussed what can happen if a family does not have a good plan in place to prevent generational wealth from being depleted and the family business ceasing to exist. Those pitfalls are everywhere for VHNWI and UHNWI families. But you and your family do not have to fall victim to them. There are actions you can take right now in prevention.

You can start by scheduling weekly meetings to discuss the family business, as it pertains to each member. This should be a part of your family structure. Building business plans and having multiple ideas to execute both personal goals and future business goals allows everyone an opportunity to add their creative thought process to the mix. Determining strengths and working on weak areas allow an opportunity for all to grow and expand in their role.

When you discuss personal plans, like vacation fun, and relaxing together outside the office as a family, hopefully, this enhances the camaraderie at the office. Many large companies take the entire team on a retreat to promote unity while exercising team building, ongoing conversations, fun, relaxation, and reward for jobs well done. These combine to create a positive experience, add harmony, and solidify support and commitment to a shared purpose and growth, which generally promotes all-around fulfillment. Your family should be included in this. After all, the day will come when they take the reins of the company.

Documenting such events on the corporate site, internal intranet, newsletters, will create a permanent and memorable way to mark the annual event that family members can look back on and look forward to in the future. This will boost morale and provide avenues of good communication between members. It will also provide the atmosphere needed to allow questions to be presented and fresh ideas to find a welcoming place to be heard. By doing these activities, you are building the environment needed to enhance and embrace growth. Showing leadership includes exhibiting empathy, allowing personal and family development and growth, providing the opportunity for teamwork, and continuing to emphasize and cultivate a family's purpose.

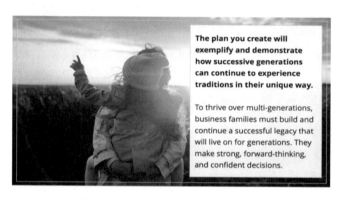

The plan you create will exemplify and demonstrate how successive generations can continue to experience traditions in their unique way.

To thrive over multi-generations, business families must build and continue a successful legacy that will live on for generations. They make strong, forward-thinking, and confident decisions.

The plan you create will exemplify and demonstrate how successive generations can continue to make the experience a tradition in their unique way. To thrive over multi-generations, business families must create and continue a tradition, a successful legacy that will live on for generations. They make strong, forward-thinking, and confident decisions. Keep in mind that principles and high standards are the cornerstones of success. A sustainable legacy begins in family reflection.

Commit to the Mission

Having a mission statement helps define and comprehend what it has represented over generations and what it means to continue it into the future. Understanding the power of the legacy helps the family business influence the world over time. Long-lasting family businesses are very mindful to avoid the entrapment and often the superficial pitfalls of success. Many are all too aware of how fleeting success and wealth can be. Hard work, planning, devotion, listening, engaging with an open heart and mind, and skilled communication are key to continued generational success.

Strong business and family values and morals can and should have a long-term impact on each person through the generations. It is important to understand that these strong generational values need to be taught and developed early on. With great wealth comes great privilege, and the most valuable lesson you can teach your children, at a very young age, is that they, too, must earn their way up through the family business and life. Keeping a child grounded in their life, even for the very wealthy, will keep them from overindulgence, and it will demonstrate their value and the importance of decision making.

Mentoring a child to become an adult with great responsibilities and wealth takes dedication and balance. If they do not see the dedication to work, then all they may see is excess, and all they may do is seek ways to fill their days with excess. The drive to succeed comes from needing to succeed. If it is handed down on a silver platter, unfortunately, we are all too aware of the entitlement that some have been given. We have seen it splashed across tabloids and on social media as to how inherited wealth without the need for hard work often leads to a lack of true fulfillment. That void is often filled with distractions that include drugs, alcohol, and a life full of excess, without the work. Yes, it may all seem like fun, but if it continues, they need to be taught responsibility that led up to having fun. It is crucial to recognize, appreciate and pass along the values inherited from previous generations in the family. Only then will each generation instill that unto the next generation of family members and employees.

Continuing to build your family legacy means teaching and exhibiting the inherent morals and values that came before you. It includes more than just building wealth; it includes expounding upon your family's values. Many families have taken to making a documentary about generational success as it came to be. Interviewing how a founding patriarch or matriarch began with having nothing, to become an entrepreneur who successfully launched a family business is a compelling way to tell your family story. The founding generation often came from humble beginnings and struggled for years to make their life a success. It's important for the family legacy that the family understands the greatest accomplishments, their most challenging times, and how they recognized opportunities or overcame great challenges or hardship.

Continuing to build your family legacy means teaching and exhibiting the inherent morals and values that came before you.

It includes more than just creating wealth; it expounds upon your family's values.

When speaking passionately about their values, direction, and vision, they hope that future generations will follow. Their life's mission can be sustained through their children and their children's children. Each generation should follow suit in adding to this documentary that will record their history, the progress, the ideas, and the perseverance that went into the family business. Recording the success and including the challenges faced gives the future generation directives to follow, long after the original and succeeding generations are gone. A well-made movie (perhaps filmed by a documentary producer who will gather the extended family to help craft questions) can help the younger generation to feel intimately connected to the past while learning directly from the founder and subsequent successors, more about the instrumental and fundamental ways in which their wisdom helped lead the way into the future. Sure, the situations and times change, but the fortitude, ingenuity, and powerful desire to continue the legacy will hopefully continue. Consider the importance a record of your family business history has on paper. It is more inspiring to create a video to be kept in perpetuity and continually add new key members' stories to share the important ways they were raised, mentored, and groomed toward succession.

In creating a movie of how your family's highly successful business began and by including both the opportunities and the challenges, the dedication along with the thoughts behind the decision-making skills that helped to continue the legacy, you are passing along your knowledge in a way that will mean more than just reading it, or even just listening to it, because seeing it on a screen, makes a greater impact. In every generation, there is a time, be it a war, a shortage of materials, a labor issue, pandemics, catastrophic obstacles that have occurred on every leader's watch. Include the thinking, the solutions, and the pivotal moments that tough decisions were made that most companies have had to make at one time or another. This testament will guide the next generation to understand that success did not just "happen" in most cases.

The Benefits of Working in a Family Business

The many benefits of working in a family business can be incredibly worthwhile. For example, it is extremely exciting to see our children growing up to take over the business, and it is even more exciting when they bring in innovative ideas. They are part of the family, and it is important for them to feel like they belong as they contribute to its success.

When your employees understand the "why" behind their being asked to do something, it helps to stress how important their input is. This is especially true for families in business together. Sharing your vision of success with the entire team allows everyone to align with that same vision, no matter how large or small a part they may play.

Sharing your vision of success with the entire family allows everyone to align with that same vision, no matter how large or small a part they may play.

This type of thinking was exemplified by those such as Steve Jobs. Something he learned from his father struck him and remained important to him. Steve passed on this "philosophy" to his engineers. Even though nobody would see the inside of Apple products, except for repair people, Steve wanted the engineers to understand the "why" of what they were doing and be proud of it. Steve had a perfectionist point of view that related to his passion. According to Walter Isaacson, his authorized biographer, while at the helm of Apple, Jobs insisted that every element of the Macintosh computer be beautiful, down to the circuit boards inside.

"Look at the memory chips. That's ugly. The lines are too close together," Jobs said of the circuits in Isaacson's biography. When the computer was finally perfected, Jobs had the engineers' sign their names engraved inside each one." Real artists sign their work, he told them, and while no one would ever see the signatures, the members of the team knew that their signatures were inside, just as they knew that the circuit board was laid out as elegantly as possible," according to the book.[5]

You Must Prioritize Family

We all hope that our values, ideals, and work ethics have been evident as we raised our children while we worked diligently at the same time. Finding a balance between our work life and family life is never easy. And often, of course, we think we may have succeeded, the younger generation may not have the same perspective. Some of the second generation may or may not have taken on our traits. As

[5] Ali_Montag. (2018, May 10). *Steve Jobs learned this brilliant lesson about success as a teen, building a fence with his dad.* CNBC. Retrieved March 26, 2022, from https://www.cnbc.com/2018/05/10/ how-steve-jobs-developed-his-design-philosophy-for-apple.html

individuals and like most generations, they are more impacted by their peers than their parents. But we, as parents, can help change that and this starts with a balanced work and family life.

The importance of balance is well noted by the imbalance in Steve Jobs' family life. He had a work ethic that brought him great wealth, and his legacy will live on, but not necessarily through future generations of his family due to his lack of not having strong, solid family relations. Yes, Apple is a highly successful company, but in the end, he held only a small percentage of the company, and his executives took the helm. While leaving a legacy behind for sure, it was not a successful family legacy. None of his family are involved in his business, and the wealth his wife inherited, now worth close to twenty-two billion, will not be passed along to the next generation. Some families do not believe in generational wealth transfer, and from the little we know, his business sense is not something he taught his children. It's saddening that none of his four children have fond memories of him or hold him in high esteem as a father.

One of the most important roles you can take on is a role model, a parent, a mentor, a guide to the next generation to help them pay it forward. Work-life balance plays a significant role in life and business for future generations to come. Generational wealth can also be generational disfunction. We are here to guide you to make the decisions that will lead to total fulfillment in those areas. I guarantee Jobs did not leave this earth, wishing he had spent more time at the office.

How we converse with the ones we love makes a tremendous difference.

Managing your Family Dynamics

As parents, our first and the utmost of all responsibilities is the protection of our children. That includes our relationships and familial bonds with our children and even their children, in order to protect the family for years to come.

As previously discussed, guidance, nurturing, and leadership must be exhibited in both your family and your workplace with the goal in the ability to protect the relationships within both. Family members are often at the heart of our closest yet most intense source of stress and disagreements. Because of this, it is important to try and sustain a healthy relationship. How we simply converse with the ones we love makes a great difference.

By far the main priority for all involved is open-minded communication. While you maintain a business relationship, you must also remember to support the personal relationship, which does have a distinct set of boundaries. While you may want to discuss the nitty-gritty of the business and its role within the organization, it is not appropriate to cross the line into the nitty-gritty aspects of their personal lives. In many families, that line becomes blurred because personal lives can often enormously impact the business.

It is often where a third, objective party can often help. A business manager, a financial wealth advisor, or a business consultant life coach can often help mediate when family issues, divorce, illness, substance abuse are all things that may cross over to impact the daily performance in your business. This can unintentionally cause additional stress and strains on the family dynamic. Most family members have their own lives, which have personal and financial obligations, social interactions, time constraints, investment needs, health issues, and an additional set of in-laws on top of that. Those factors create layers that impact family members and employees, executives, and board members. It has a substantial impact in this ever-changing world and needs to be considered when it affects the family and the business.

Wealth Transition and Succession Planning

As we said earlier, a sustaining legacy begins in family reflection. A mission statement helps define and comprehend what it has represented in the past and what it means to take it into the future. When followed, it can assist every family member in staying on the same page, remaining on track, and so they are reading from the same book. Succession's transition depends on it.

The transition of the family business often also includes a transition of wealth. The past two years have altered the thinking of many people. During the pandemic, people took a closer look at what they deemed to be extremely important in their lives. Some families placed more focus on different areas than others.

At the same time, many faced the loss or compromised health of family members, both young and old, which increased awareness and emphasized succession planning and generational wealth transfer. It also brought increasing concerns about how prepared or ill-prepared the upcoming generation was to oversee the leadership in many businesses. The older generation, in many families, felt pressure to increase the preparations for the younger generation to accelerate their involvement should the timeline be shortened by health impacts or financial crisis.

It also involved the timing aspects of the younger generation, if they were still not of age, busy in college, and not ready to step up. Succession plans included a longer lens and often involved board members, non-family members, and senior executives being named to transition.

When questioned as to what keeps people awake at night when thinking about the future, many upper-middle-class families worried about inflation, the impact on their standard of living, job security, food on the table, overall health and health insurance, their children's well-being, and remote education throughout the past few stress-filled years.

For the VHNWI and the UHNWI, they too worried about their family, their overall health, the impact on their children, but close to 40% of them lay awake at night concerned about the next 12 months. They were also often concerned about succession planning. Almost 30% were concerned about wealth consumption, rising inflation, and nearly 30% were perturbed about taxes.

The fact that many are very disconcerted about the challenge of readying the next generation for leadership is an overall concern that keeps close to 40% of business leaders staring at the ceiling late at night and means that much of their anxiety need to be carefully addressed. The anxieties about their family's future plagued them, but there are things to alleviate some of those fears. Those fears should be tackled early on.

As discussed previously, involving the family in business and philanthropic endeavors can start early in a child's life. Generally, a true succession is when the older generation (Gen 1) is ready to retire or take a step back from the business to focus more on philanthropic endeavors. It takes years of mentoring and training the younger generation Gen 2 (ages 25 to 40-year-olds) to take the reins. The actual transition may take 3 to 5 years of planning and costs more than one thinks regarding time preparation, finances, and the emotional toll involved. When multiple children are involved in the family business, the succession plan takes careful balance and often requires outside objective assistance. This process can help prevent miscommunication, misunderstandings, and promotes fair and wise plans where the family and business are concerned.

Ensure that communication remains open and that the mission statement and corporate values are aligned. That allows for an easier succession. However, consider that the younger generations have more interest in technology, apps, portals, sharing information online, or in a seven or eight-second summation on a screen, or in short podcasts, which affords them to work within their timeframe. They may listen in on a recorded meeting after it happens if they are tied up with a more prominent issue. It allows the technological innovation that has impacted business greatly to continue improving and addressing the message, mission, and legacy that a generational business has had while actively listening and allowing the new generation to incorporate growing technology.

Following the shared mission, looking back to past family/corporate retreats, understanding the goals and visions that created a successful empire helps everyone to remain focused and on task as to the desired outcome and will remain an important part of success during a thoughtful succession/transition plan. It will also provide ways to make memories, find inner peace, and enjoy the next chapter of your life. Feeling content in knowing that your family's legacy is in good hands will do wonders in you finding happiness after succession.

Leadership, Governance, and Decision Making

It is imperative to have a sturdy foundation to allow for trust, communication, and structure to make sound and effective decisions within your inner sphere. Your overall decisions will impact your family's business, generational wealth, and continued well-being. Making important decisions while setting standards by following the original common and shared mission and changing future technologies is important.

Not surprisingly, most family conglomerates have the top-down mentality. This translates into the older generation, while of sound mind and in control, are often the ones that "decides and makes unilateral judgment calls" to carry out his wishes. Those wishes are often looked upon as demands by the next generation.

We had previously discussed that the younger generation might be more adept in newer, more innovative areas such as technology. They may have a shorter attention span and are more in tune with how the next generation will be operating into the future. The successful family builds trust among its family members across multi-generations and is honest and willingly open to assigning the roles where the family member has strengths, where they belong and excel rather than taking complete control and dictating authority in an area, they may not exhibit expertise. A solid, well-communicative family understands that most members have certain strengths in areas and constraints in others. A wise leader helps members grow their strengths rather than focus on areas of weakness or constraints. When the goals support the overall mission, the trust members have with each other will support its overall success and help keep peace among the family as they move forward together. A division of thinking, or trust, creates a dysfunctional team and family and can lead the corporation and the family to suffer great loss.

Successful governance has a guide and a set of principles for all members, family, and employees to follow. This guide should incorporate the following practices and procedures and should be done as members of a team:

1. Define the objectives and challenges.

2. Fully research the data from multiple sources.

3. Evaluate all the data gained.

4. Discuss several viable solutions and the potential outcomes of each with your team, including both the positive and negative potential.

5. Set the KPI standards by which to evaluate its success.

6. Narrow down the solutions to choose the best one and execute it.

7. Closely evaluate and continue to monitor the KPI's after the solution has been in place for a predetermined timeframe.

8. If the solution is successful, that should be recorded as part of the history. If it is unsuccessful, different steps and exercises must be performed again, until a successful outcome is achieved.

It is important to note the success and failures as there is much to be learned from both going forward for future generations.

Remaining healthy and of a clear mind remains consistent with going forward in life and business with a healthy outlook.

Remember, by passing along the protocols and outcomes, you are setting the governing affairs for future generational success to follow the path and teaching them the "why and how." This allows for a deeper understanding of the shared values that came before them.

Personal Mental and Physical Health for your Family

The age-old saying that money cannot buy health or happiness, but it sure can help, does hold true. Maintaining your mental and physical health is what we can only do for ourselves. Leading a life with mindfulness, eating well and healthfully, doing everything in moderation instead of in excess can be easier than many think. While great wealth can buy many things and give you access to outstanding health care, it cannot buy your health and peace of mind.

Remaining humble, down-to-earth, focused on doing good things for others now and in the future give much meaning and adds fulfillment to life. Mental well-being is very tied in with our physical well-being, and our physical well-being impacts our mental status. Taking care of your physical self takes maintaining good schedules for sleep, meals, regular exercise, positive attitudes, and maintaining a health-conscious lifestyle. Annual or semi-annual physicals, complete with bloodwork and any scans, are important, as well as listening to your body if something seems out of sorts to follow up and check it out. Many have ignored their health for the past two years due to the pandemic. It is important not to let your healthcare lapse. For those who have mental or physical ailments or family members who are not mindful, seeking professional help is important. Remaining healthy and of a clear mind remains consistent with going forward in life and business with a healthy outlook.

Preparation for a Crisis

Once the pandemic struck, many businesses globally went remote, and meetings have been held virtually, including family meetings. While, initially, this was thought to be a temporary change, it has quickly become obvious to many businesses that anything can be done remotely.

The world has recently overcome many obstacles out of necessity. Now, more than ever, the virtual trend has led us more toward globalized business. Many only go into the office once a week and can work virtually from anywhere in the world.

By the time a catastrophe occurs, in many cases, the time to prepare for it has passed. This evidence became quite clear during the pandemic when paper towels, toilet paper, masks, and laptops for working at their home office and home-school learning became major obstacles to overcome.

National and global disruptions occur without notice, creating havoc in the market, the military, hospitals, and the supply chain, creating chaos that ripples throughout the world, as we have most recently experienced. Among the deepest concerns of most are market disruption, the continuous threat of cybersecurity, the possibility of the geopolitical environment causing havoc, and concerns about the financial recession. A paper towel and toilet paper shortage created panic, and people stockpiled on dry and canned goods. A ship caught in the Suez Canal blocked the international trade route and halted global shipping operations! Food shelves were emptied in tremendous panic buying because of the lack of supply chain operations.

Shelter

During a disaster, finding safe shelter may be crucial. Whether you have a safe room in your home or have a secondary safe place, you can determine if heading there is necessary. Food supplies, cash, and medication should be set up in advance. If several different family members congregate there, figure out in advance how they will get there logistically and have a plan B for everyone, should that be necessary. Whether sheltering at a residence or business facility, the family should evaluate and establish a relationship with a local physician with core ER competency.

Communication

A detailed manual and a digital copy should be available and ready to implement for all family members at home, on vacation, or at office locations. The annual family meeting or retreat is an ideal time to discuss, amend and update any changes due to the family dynamics.

Create a group text or secure an app just for emergency purposes. The group should be aside from any normal business communication and be set in motion only during an emergency. Consider that during 9/11 and some major hurricanes, fires, or earthquakes, many cellular networks are overloaded, and a text message is more likely to succeed when Wi-Fi and cellular systems are down. Satellite communications should remain up during an event, so coordinate satellite communications and establish them at your business or residence. When living or traveling abroad, verify access communication in advance with local consulates/embassy. Have the location and all contact information; they are an intricate part of obtaining information in an emergency, whether to provide medical assistance or evacuation information.

Medical Concerns

Coordinating this in advance is necessary and having access to telemedicine or concierge medicine is something many families already have set in place. Think about not having immediate access to doctors or a pharmacy for medicine. Your family health records, including information on existing medical conditions and current medications, should be kept both in hard copy and digitally. A medication stock should be stored and rotated out to ensure the dates have not expired. Have medical equipment, such as a C-PAP machine and oxygen if needed. If someone has a heart condition, besides medication, a handheld EKG device and defibrillator in the house are appropriate to carry.

Familiarize yourself and family members in the operation direction before an emergency and review it annually or more frequently if needed. During a crisis, the response to a 911 call may not be answered, so having expertise in managing needed equipment is a good plan to put in place. Of course, the same goes for stocking enough food and water, canned and dry foods, and equipment to function such as a can opener, camp stove, and enough supplies, including fuel for up to a month or more, to run a generator in the event of an emergency.

Energy

A backup generator should be located at your home, safe shelter, and office. Storing large quantities of gasoline with a stabilizer may remain fresh for about a year, but propane provides a more efficient fuel source and is safer to store. An electrician should set it up initially and teach family members, including responsible children, to be trained how to power it on and switch it onto generator mode. Monthly or quarterly test runs with several family members (that last 5 to 10 minutes) should be done to make certain of your comfort level in startup and proactively make certain the generator/battery is in good running order to power your appliances directly. Fuel should be safely stored away from the residence.

Security Concerns

Security guidelines should long be in place at your level of success. Emergency contingencies for any cyber-attacks, especially during a crisis, is crucial because there is always an uptick in both cyber and criminal behavior during a disaster. Whenever chaos, panic, or disruption occurs, you must be on high alert before opening any communications. Be certain all incoming information is from legitimate sources. Intrusion occurs when access is gained from what appears to be a safe, known source. However, many trusted sources are intended to look that way when addresses or links look similar but are not exact. Opening such an email gives access to your digital resources, including passwords, accounts, etc. Instruct your family not to open anything unless they have verified the source by checking the full address. Have them ask, before opening, if they are unsure. Do not click on any links that may look suspicious as they may contain malware that will create havoc.

Conclusion

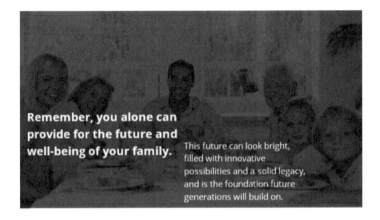

Remember, you alone can provide for the future and well-being of your family. This future can look bright, filled with innovative possibilities and a solid legacy, and is the foundation future generations will build on.

Remember, you alone can provide for the future and wellbeing of your family. This future can continue to look bright, filled with innovative possibilities, a legacy that is solid and is the foundation for many generations to come to build upon. You can start today to build for future tomorrows that continue the success of your family personally and in business. You can avoid many pitfalls found in living and navigating generations of wealth.

Please consider our one-on-one Guiding **the Next Generation to Thrive and Build Continued Success for Your Family Legacy coaching program.**

We understand that your family has unique needs and goals, and our coaching program is tailored to meet those needs.

This book was written to help guide those who strive for more. We hope the topics discussed here will assist you on that journey. Setting your goals, thinking about what your vision of success looks like, has most likely been incorporated into your life for a long time now because you have reached this pinnacle in your life. Passing that along to the future generations is important, and setting the wheels in motion for continued generations to follow in your path is a goal that bring much happiness, pride, and continued success.

The journey is not always easy, but it is well worth the effort. If you desire to continue the conversation, feel free to reach out based on your situation. We are happy to listen and offer our services to assist you.

To work together on your journey and continued success, please visit our website at MillionaireLife.Services or choose a self-paced online course or our membership plan at MillionaireLifeServices.uteach.io. Our courses are designed to empower you with the knowledge and skills you need to achieve your goals. Our courses and membership plans are designed to help you strengthen your family and protect your legacy.

Cliff K. Locks

Chief Learning and Succession Officer for family enterprises, Executive Strategy Life Consultant, Professional Coach, Serial Entrepreneur, and Board Advisor

https://MillionaireLife.Services

About the Author

Cliff Locks is a Chief Learning and Succession Officer for family enterprises and an Executive Strategy Life Consultant, Professional Coach, Serial Entrepreneur, and Board Advisor. He has an abundance of experience helping executives, business leaders, and family offices achieve their goals and unlock their full potential in both their professional and personal lives.

For decades, Cliff has been a trusted advisor to high-level clients. He has providing one-on-one leadership, lifestyle and executive strategy, and business coaching services. He also specializes in guiding the next generation to thrive and build continued success, with deep expertise in preparing next-generation family members for succession in the family enterprise.

Using a personal and individualized approach to each engagement, Cliff tailors his services to fit each client's unique needs and circumstances, thereby empowering them to fully achieve their highest aspirations.

You can learn more about his work and services at https://MillionaireLife.Services.

In addition to his author works, Cliff is the co-host of the Private Equity Profits Podcast, where he interviews seasoned experts managing $30 million to $3 billion in AUM. The podcast is available on multiple platforms, including podcasts.apple.com and iheart.com, providing additional insights and perspectives from some of the most successful leaders in the industry.

Learn more at:

MillionaireLife.Services

MillionaireLifeServices.uteach.io

More Products by This Author

Elevate your path to success by discovering a range of valuable resources offered by this accomplished author. Explore a selection of books, self-paced courses, and exclusive coaching and mentoring programs designed to help you achieve your goals. Additionally, unlock the potential of joining an exclusive membership for high achievers to support you and your family on its successful journey to increased greatness and positive legacy. Don't miss out on the opportunity to take your success to the next level with the guidance and expertise of this accomplished author.

Other products by this author include:

1. Key Strategies to Encourage Your Children to Succeed and Learn to Flourish Independently (Book and Course)

2. Guiding the Next Generation to Thrive and Build Continued Success for Your Family Legacy (Book you are currently reading and Course)

3. Mastering Anger: Understanding and Managing Your Emotions (Book and Course)

4. Emerging Leaders Program – The Basics and More for Becoming a Successful and Great Leader (Course)

5. Executive Leadership Academy – Practical Leadership Skills: Unlocking Your Full Potential (Course)

6. Millionaire Life Services Next Generation and Family Enterprise Executive Coaching (Membership)

7. Achieving Success at an Accelerated Speed: Learn How to Hit Goals at Superhuman Speeds by Harnessing the Power of Thoughts and Calculated Actions (Book and Course)

8. How to Achieve Success Fast - Learn How to Hit Goals by Harnessing the Power of

Your Thoughts and Calculated Action (Book)

9. 14 Secrets of Success to Become a Self-Made Millionaire (Course)

10. How to be a Self-Made Millionaire: What Are the Secrets of Success? (Book)

These books can be found on Amazon.com.

Please note that the publishing schedule will determine the availability of the printed books and Kindle edition, but all courses are currently accessible.

These courses and membership can be found on MillionaireLifeServices.uteach.io.

All courses are online and self-paced; pick up right where you left off and never lose your place with automatic progress tracking.

Made in the USA
Columbia, SC
11 January 2024

30275708R00054